MY AUNT JANE AUSTEN

Jane Austen's Memorial Trust

Jane Austen's House, Chawton

MY AUNT JANE AUSTEN

A MEMOIR

BY

CAROLINE AUSTEN

THE JANE AUSTEN SOCIETY

First Published in Great Britain 1952
by the Jane Austen Society
New Edition 1991
Reprinted 1999, 2008

ISBN 978-095-1103-531

Printed by Sarsen Press, 22 Hyde Street, Winchester

CONTENTS

PREFACE

CAROLINE MARY CRAVEN AUSTEN was the daughter, by his second wife, of Jane Austen's eldest brother, James. She was born in 1805, and was thus seven years younger than her brother James Edward, (always called Edward), who in 1837 became Austen-Leigh, and later his aunt's first biographer. Caroline's half-sister Anna Lefroy was James's only child by his first wife. Edward's and Caroline's mother was Mary Lloyd, whose sister Martha lived with Mrs. Austen and her daughters at Southampton and later at Chawton.

Caroline's recollections were quoted in the *Memoir* of 1870 and in the *Life and Letters* of 1913, and are printed almost complete in *Personal Aspects of Jane Austen* by Mary Augusta Austen-Leigh (1920). They depend partly on her retentive memory, partly on what she elsewhere calls "my mother's well-kept pocket-books".

The document is valuable for the facts it has preserved. It is more remarkable for its own sake. The introduction, with its vivid picture of "the village churchyard", strikes just the right opening note. The little touches that build up the picture—the "nonsense", the invented stories, the reading that "was like a play"—are precisely what was wanted in 1867 and is wanted today.

The topographical part has little that is not familiar to anyone who has visited Chawton. It is worth noting that the "Cottage" was not then so called; and indeed its "affluence of space" deserved a larger name. My guess is that it was called the Small House, for Chawton Manor is in Jane Austen's letters always the Great House. Readers of them will recall the "very considerable pond"[1] and the "six bed-chambers".[2]

The account of the family needs little further comment than I have given above. "Cassy", so distinguished from other Cassandras,[3] is Jane's "that puss Cassy"[4]; her mother had died in 1814.

[1] 9 July 1816. [2] 21 Nov. 1808.

[3] The name was traditional in Mrs. Austen's (née Leigh) family.

[4] 30 Nov. 1814.

Mary Jane is Frank Austen's eldest daughter. There are a few references to persons not named. The "cousin long since dead", who found his visits after Jane's death a "disappointment", was probably a son of one of the sailor brothers (both Captains at the period described, but later Admirals). Virtually the same story is told of "a nephew" in the *Memoir*, and it has been assumed (e.g. by myself) following the *Life and Letters* that the writer described his own experience. But we must probably conclude that he was quoting Caroline. The brother who is described as Jane's "especial pride and delight" must I think be Henry, though he, alone of the family, was sometimes a cause of anxiety. His bankruptcy, which he bore with cheerfulness, cost one of his brothers a large sum of money; this no doubt underlies Caroline's allusion to "forbearance and generosity" needed to preserve the "firm family union".

But the essence of Caroline's modest story is in the picture of Aunt Jane, a nonpareil of aunts. We have long known her own high opinion of that status and function.

"His having been in love with the Aunt, gives Cecilia[1] an additional Interest. I like the Idea:—a very proper compliment to an Aunt! I rather imagine indeed that Neices are seldom chosen but in compliment to some Aunt or other!"[2]

"Now that you have become an Aunt, you are a person of some consequence . . . I have always maintained the importance of Aunts."[3]

To this self-portrait we can now add a pendant in the equally sympathetic picture of an Aunt as seen by a niece. Yet people go on telling us that Jane Austen disliked children.

Caroline's remarks on her aunt's letters are of hardly less interest. She understood, what so many critics have missed, the essential point, that the letters are nearly all family letters, intended to be read by or to all members of the family who might be in the house to which they were sent; she saw therefore that "to strangers they could be no transcript of her mind". It is to Caroline that we owe the sad knowledge that Cassandra destroyed such

[1] A fictional character.
[2] Dec. 1814.
[3] 30 Oct. 1815.

letters to herself as "were, I dare say,[1] open and confidential". We have no right to complain. But we may regret the necessity of piecing together Jane's love-story from odds and ends of distant recollection.

Of her aunt as author Caroline has little to tell beyond some engaging particulars of her way of work. She enlarges, indeed, on the Regent's appreciation and affability. But that story was already better told in the letters and in that exquisite piece of fooling, *Plan of a Novel according to Hints from Various Quarters.*

R. W. CHAPMAN.

[1] "I dare say" meant, at that time, "I am quite sure".

Joan Austen-Leigh

Caroline Austen as a child

MY AUNT JANE AUSTEN

A MEMOIR of Miss Jane Austen has often been asked for, and strangers have declared themselves willing and desirous to undertake the task of writing it—and have wondered that the family should have refused to supply the necessary materials. But tho' none of the nearest relatives desired that the details of a very private and rather uneventful life should be laid before the world yet I think they would not willingly have had her memory die—and it will die and be lost, if no effort is made to preserve it—The grass grave in the village churchyard sinks down in a few years to the common level, and its place is no more to be found and so, to keep the remembrance of the departed a little longer in the world which they have left, we lay a stone over their graves, and inscribe upon it their name and age, and perhaps some few words of their virtues and of our own sorrow—and tho' the stone moulders and tho' the letters fade away, yet do they outlast the interest of what they record—We remember our dead always—but when we shall have joined them their memory may be said to have perished out of the earth—for no distinct idea of them remains behind, and the next generation soon forget that they ever existed—

For most of us therefore, the memorial on the perishing tombstone is enough—and more than enough—it will tell its tale longer than anyone will care to read it—But not so for all—Every country has had its great men, whose lives have been and are still read—with unceasing interest; and so, in *some* families there has been *one* distinguished by talent or goodness, and known far beyond the home circle, whose memory ought to be preserved through more than a single generation—Such a one was my Aunt—Jane Austen—

Since her death, the public voice has placed her in the first rank of the Novellists of her day—given her, I may say, the first place amongst them—and it seems but right that *some* record should remain with *us* of her life and character; and that *she* herself should not be forgotten by her nearest descendants, whilst her writings still *live,* and are still spreading her fame wherever the English books are read.—Her last long surviving Brother has recently died at the age of 91 (1865)—The generation who knew her is passing away—but those who are succeeding us must feel an interest in the personal character of their Great Aunt, who has made the family name in some small degree, illustrious—For them therefore, and for my own gratification I will try to call back my recollections of what she was, and what manner of life she led—It is not much that I have to tell—for I mean to relate only what I saw and what I *thought* myself—I was just twelve years old when she died—therefore, I knew her only with a child's knowledge—

My first very distinct remembrance of her is in her own home at Chawton—The house belonged to her second brother, Mr. Knight (of Godmersham & Chawton) and was by him made a comfortable residence for his mother and sisters—The family party there were, my grandmother, Mrs. Austen—my two aunts, her daughters—and a third aunt of mine—Miss Lloyd, who had made her home with them before I can remember, and who remained their inmate as long as Mrs. Austen lived—

The dwelling place of a favourite author always possesses a certain interest for those who love the books that issued from it—Tho' some of my aunt's novels were imagined and written in her very early days—*some* certainly at Steventon yet it was from Chawton that after being rearranged and prepared for publication they were sent out into the world—and it is with Chawton therefore, that her name as an author, must be identified—The house which she inhabited was in itself, not much more deserving of notice than Cowper's dwelling place at Olney—and yet more than 30 years after his death, that was pointed out to us, as a something that strangers passing through the little town, must wish to see—Now, as the remembrance of Chawton Cottage, for so in later years it came to be called, is still pleasant to me—I will assume that those who never knew it, may like to have laid before them, a description of their Aunt's home—the last that she dwelt in—where, in the maturity of her mind, she completed the works that have given her an *English* name—where after a few years, whilst still in the prime of life, she began to droop and wither away—the home from whence she removed only in the last stage of her illness, by the persuasion of her friends, hoping against hope —and to which her sister before long had to return alone—

My Grand Father, Mr. Austen, held for many years, the adjoining livings of Deane and Steventon—but gave up his duties to his eldest son, and settled at Bath, a very few years before his own death—For a while, his widow and daughters remained at Bath —then they removed to Southampton—and finally settled in the village of Chawton—

Mr. Knight had been able to offer his mother the choice of two houses—one in Kent near to Godmersham—and the other at Chawton—and she and her daughters eventually decided on the Hampshire residence.

I have been told I know not how truthfully, that it had been originally a roadside Inn—and it was well placed for such a purpose—just where the road from Winchester comes into the London and Gosport line—The fork between the two being partly occupied by a large shallow pond—which pond I beleive has long since become dry ground—

The front door opened on the road, a very narrow enclosure of each side protected the house from the possible shock of any runaway vehicle—A good sized entrance, and two parlours called dining and drawing room, made the length of the house; all intended originally to look on the road—but the large drawing room window was blocked-up and turned into a bookcase when Mrs. Austen took possession and another was opened at the side, which gave to view only turf and trees—a high wooden fence shut out the road (the Winchester road it was) all the length of the little domain, and trees were planted inside to form a shrubbery walk—which carried round the enclosure, gave a very sufficient space for exercise—you did not feel cramped for room; and there was a pleasant irregular mixture of hedgerow, and grass, and gravel walk and long grass for mowing, and orchard—which I imagine arose from two or three little enclosures having been thrown together, and arranged as best might be, for ladies' occupation—There was besides a good kitchen garden, large court and many out-buildings, not much occupied—and all this affluence of space was very delightful to children, and I have no doubt added considerably to the pleasure of a visit—

Everything indoors and *out* was well kept—the house was well furnished, and it was altogether a comfortable and ladylike establishment, tho' I beleive the means which supported it, were but small—

The house was quite as good as the generality of Parsonage houses then—and much in the same old style—the ceilings low and roughly finished—*some* bedrooms very small—*none* very large but in number sufficient to accomodate the inmates, and several guests—

The dining room could not be made to look anywhere but on the road—and there my grandmother often sat for an hour or two in the morning, with her work or her writing—cheered by its sunny aspect and by the stirring scene it afforded her.

I beleive the close vicinity of the road was really no more an evil to her than it was to her grandchildren. Collyer's daily coach with six horses was a sight to see! and most delightful was it to a child to have the awful stillness of night so frequently broken by the noise of passing carriages, which seemed sometimes, even to shake the bed—

The village of Chawton has, of course, long since been tranquilised—it is no more a great thoroughfare, and *other* and *many* changes have past over it—and if any of its visitants should fail to recognise from my description, the house by the pond—I must beg them not hastily to accuse me of having exaggerated its former pleasantness.

Twenty years ago, on being then left vacant by Aunt Cassandra's death, it was divided into habitations for the poor, and made to accomodate several families—so I was *told*—for I have never seen it since and I beleive trees have been cut down, and all that could be termed pleasure ground has reverted again to more ordinary purposes—

My visits to Chawton were frequent—I cannot tell *when* they began—they were very pleasant to me—and Aunt Jane was the great charm—As a very little girl, I was always creeping up to her, and following her whenever I could, in the house and out of it—I might not have remembered this, but for the recollection of my mother's telling me privately, I must not be troublesome to my aunt—

Her charm to children was great sweetness of manner—she seemed to love you, and you loved her naturally in return—*This* as well as I can now recollect and analyse, was what I felt in my earliest days, before I was old enough to be amused by her cleverness—But soon came the delight of her playful talk—*Every-thing* she could make amusing to a child—Then, as I got older, and when cousins came to share the entertainment, she would tell us the most delightful stories chiefly of Fairyland, and her Fairies had all characters of their own—The tale was invented, I am sure, at the moment, and was sometimes continued for 2 or 3 days, if occasion served—

As to my Aunt's personal appearance, her's was the first face that I can remember thinking pretty, not that I used that word to myself, but I know I looked at her with admiration—Her face was rather round than long—she had a bright, but not a pink colour—a clear brown complexion and very good hazle eyes—She was not, I beleive, an absolute beauty, but before she left Steventon she was established as a very pretty girl, in the opinion of most of her neighbours—as I learned afterwards from some of those who still remained—Her hair, a darkish brown, curled naturally—it was in short curls round her face (for *then* ringlets were *not*.) She always wore a cap—Such was the custom with ladies who were not quite young—at least of a morning but I never saw her without one, to the best of my remembrance, either morning or evening.

I beleive my two Aunts were not accounted very good dressers, and were thought to have taken to the garb of middle age unnecessarily soon—but they were particularly neat, and they held all untidy ways in great disesteem. Of the two, Aunt Jane was by far my favourite—I did not *dislike* Aunt Cassandra—but if my visit had at any time chanced to fall out during *her* absence, I don't think I should have missed her—whereas, *not* to have found Aunt Jane at Chawton, *would* have been a blank indeed.

As I grew older, I met with young companions at my Grandmother's—Of Capt. Charles Austen's motherless girls, *one* the eldest, Cassy—lived there chiefly, for a time—under the especial tutorage of Aunt Cassandra; and then Chawton House was for a while inhabited by Capt. Frank Austen; and *he* had many children —I beleive we were all of us, according to our different ages and natures, very fond of our Aunt Jane—and that we ever retained a strong impression of the pleasantness of Chawton life—One of my cousins, now long since dead, after he was grown up, used occasionally to go and see Aunt Cass—*then* left sole inmate of the old house—and he told me once, that his visits were always a disappointment to him—for that he could not help expecting to feel particularly happy at Chawton and never till he got there, could he fully realise to himself how all its peculiar pleasures were gone—

In the time of my childhood, it was a cheerful house—my Uncles, one or another, frequently coming for a few days; and they were all pleasant in their own family—I have thought since, after having seen more of other households, *wonderfully*, as the family talk had much of spirit and vivacity, and it was never troubled by disagreements as it was not their habit to argue with each other—There always was perfect harmony amongst the brothers and sisters, and over my Grandmother's door might have been inscribed the text, "Behold how good—and joyful a thing it is, brethren, to dwell together in unity." There was firm family union, never broken but by death—tho' the time came when that union could not have been preserved if natural affection had not been by a spirit of forbearance and generosity—

Aunt Jane began her day with music—for which I conclude she had a natural taste; as she thus kept it up—tho' she had no one to teach; was never induced (as I have heard) to play in company; and none of her family cared much for it. I suppose, that she might not trouble them, she chose her practising time before breakfast—when she could have the room to herself—She practised regularly every morning—She played very pretty tunes, *I* thought—and I liked to stand by her and listen to them; but the music, (for I knew the books well in after years) would now be thought disgracefully easy—Much that she played from was manuscript, copied out by herself—and so neatly and correctly, that it was as easy to read as print—

At 9 o'clock she made breakfast—*that* was *her* part of the household work—The tea and sugar stores were under *her* charge —*and* the wine—Aunt Cassandra did all the rest—for my Grandmother had suffered herself to be superseded by her daughters *before* I can remember; and soon *after*, she ceased even to sit at the head of the table—

I don't beleive Aunt Jane observed any particular method in parcelling out her day but I think she generally sat in the drawing room till luncheon: when visitors were there, chiefly at work—She was fond of work—and she was a great adept at overcast and satin stitch—the peculiar delight of that day—General handiness and neatness were amongst her characteristics—She could throw the spilikens for us, better than anyone else, and she was wonderfully successful at cup and ball—She found a resource sometimes in that simple game, when she suffered from weak eyes and could not work or read for long together—

Her handwriting remains to bear testimony to its own excellence; and every note and letter of hers, was finished off handsomely—There was an art *then* in folding and sealing—no adhesive envelopes made all easy—some people's letters looked always loose and untidy—but *her* paper was sure to take the right folds, and *her* sealing wax to drop in the proper place—

After luncheon, my Aunts generally walked out—sometimes they went to Alton for shopping—Often, one or the other of them, to the Great House—as it was then called—when a brother was inhabiting it, to make a visit—or if the house were standing empty they liked to stroll about the grounds—sometimes to Chawton Park—a noble beech wood, just within a walk—but sometimes, but that was rarely, to call on a neighbour—They had no carriage, and their visitings did not extend far—there were a few families living in the village—but no great intimacy was kept up with any of them—they were upon *friendly* but rather *distant* terms, with all—Yet I am sure my Aunt Jane had a regard for her neighbours and felt a kindly interest in their proceedings. She liked immensely to hear all about them. They sometimes served for her amusement, but it was her own nonsense that gave zest to the gossip—She never turned *them* into ridicule—She was as far as possible from being either censorious or satirical—she never abused them or *quizzed* them—*That* was the word of the day—an ugly word, now obsolete—and the ugly practise which it bespoke, is far less prevalent now, under *any* name, than it was *then*. The laugh she occasionally raised was by imagining for her neighbours impossible contingencies—by relating in prose or verse some trifling incident coloured to her own fancy, or in writing a history of what they had said or done, that *could* deceive nobody—As an instance I would give her description of the pursuits of Miss Mills and Miss Yates—two young ladies of whom she knew next to nothing—they were only on a visit to a near neighbour but their names tempted her into rhyme—and so *on* she went—This was before *my* time. Mrs. Lefroy knows the lines better than I do—I beleive she has a copy and I shall not attempt to quote them imperfectly here. To about the same date perhaps may be referred (at least it was equally before *my* time) a few chapters which I overheard—of a mock heroic story, written between herself and one of her nieces, and I doubt *not*, at *her* instigation—If I remember rightly, it had no other foundation than their having seen a neighbour passing on the coach, without having previously known that he was going to leave home—(This I have since been told was written entirely by the niece only under her encouragement).

I did not often see my Aunt with a book in her hand, but I beleive she was fond of reading and that she *had* read and *did* read a good deal. I doubt whether she cared very much for poetry in *general*; but she was a great admirer of Crabbe, and consequently she took a keen interest in finding out *who* he was—Other contemporary writers were well-known, but *his* origen having been obscure, his name did not announce *itself*—however by diligent enquiry she was ere long able to inform the rest of the family that he held the Living of Trowbridge, and had recently married a second time—

A very warm admirer of my Aunt's writing but a stranger in England, lately made the observation that it would be most interesting to know what had been Miss Austen's opinion on the great public events of her time—a period as she rightly observed, of the greatest interest—for my Aunt must have been a young woman, able to *think*, at the time of the French Revolution. The long disastrous chapter then begun, was closed by the battle of Waterloo, two years before her death—anyone *might* naturally desire to know what part such a mind as her's had taken in the great strifes of war and policy which so disquieted Europe for more than 20 years—and yet, it was a question that had never before presented itself to me—and tho' I have *now* retraced my steps on *this* track, I have found absolutely nothing!

The general politics of the family were Tory—rather taken for granted I suppose, than discussed, as even my Uncles seldom talked about it—and in vain do I try to recall any word or expression of Aunt Jane's that had reference to public events—*Some* bias of course she *must* have had—but I can only *guess* to which quarter it inclined—Of her historical opinions I *am* able to record thus much—that she was a most loyal adherent of Charles the 1st, and that she always encouraged my youthful beleif in Mary Stuart's perfect innocence of all the crimes with which History has charged her memory—

My Aunt must have spent much time in writing—her desk lived in the drawing room. I often saw her writing letters on it, and I beleive she wrote much of her Novels in the same way—sitting with her family, when they were quite alone; but I never saw any manuscript of *that* sort, in progress—She wrote very fully to her Brothers when they were at sea, and she corresponded with many others of her family—

There is nothing in those letters which *I* have seen that would be acceptable to the public—They were very well expressed, and they must have been very interesting to those who received them—but they detailed chiefly home and family events: and she seldom committed herself *even* to an opinion—so that to strangers they could be *no* transcript of her mind—they would not feel that they knew her any the better for having read them—

They were rather *over*-cautious, for excellence—Her letters to Aunt Cassandra (for they were sometimes separated) were, I dare say, open and confidential—My Aunt looked them over and burnt the greater part, (as she told me), 2 or 3 years before her own death—She left, or gave some as legacies to the Nieces—but of those that *I* have seen, several had portions cut out—Aunt Jane was so good as frequently to write to *me*; and in addressing a child, she was perfect—

When staying at Chawton, if my two cousins, Mary Jane and Cassy were there, we often had amusements in which my Aunt was very helpful—*She* was the one to whom we always looked for help—She would furnish us with what we wanted from her wardrobe, and *she* would often be the entertaining visitor in our make beleive house—She amused us in various ways—*once* I remember in giving a conversation as between myself and my two cousins, supposed to be grown up, the day after a Ball.

As I grew older, she would talk to me more seriously of my reading, and of my amusements—I had taken early to writing verses and stories, and I am sorry to think *how* I troubled her with reading them. She was very kind about it, and always had some praise to bestow but at last she warned me against spending too much time upon them—She said—how well I recollect it! that she *knew* writing stories was a great amusement, and *she* thought a harmless one—tho' many people, she was aware, thought otherwise—but that at my age it would be bad for me to be much taken up with my own compositions—Later still—it was after she got to Winchester, she sent me a message to this effect—That if I would take her advice, I should cease writing till I was 16, and that she had herself often wished she had *read* more, and written *less*, in the corresponding years of her own life.

She was considered to read aloud remarkably well. I did not often hear her but *once* I knew her take up a volume of Evelina and read a few pages of Mr. Smith and the Brangtons and I thought it was like a play. She had a very good *speaking* voice—This was the opinion of her contemporaries—and though I did not *then* think of it as a perfection, or ever hear it observed upon, yet its tones have never been forgotten—I can recall them even now—and I *know* they *were* very pleasant.

I have spoken of the family union that prevailed amongst my Grandmother's children—Aunt Jane was a very affectionate sister to all her brothers—One of them in particular was her especial pride and delight: but of all her family, the nearest and dearest throughout her whole life was, undoubtedly her sister—her *only* sister. Aunt Cassandra was the older by 3 or 4 years, and the habit of looking up to her begun in childhood, seemed always to continue—When I was a little girl, she would frequently say to me, if opportunity offered, that Aunt Cassandra could teach everything much better than *she* could—Aunt Cass. *knew* more—Aunt Cass. could tell me better whatever I wanted to know—all which, I ever received in respectful silence—Perhaps she thought *my* mind wanted a turn in *that* direction, but I truly beleive she did always *really* think of her sister, as the superior to herself. The most perfect affection and confidence ever subsisted between them—and great and lasting was the sorrow of the survivor when the final separation was made—

My Aunt's life at Chawton, as far as I ever knew, was an easy and pleasant one—it had little variety in it, and I am not aware of any particular trials, till her own health began to fail—She stayed from home occasionally—almost entirely with the families of her different brothers—In the Autumn of 1815 she was in London, with my Uncle, Mr. Henry Austen, then living in Hans Place—and a widower—

During her visit, he was seized with low fever and became so ill that his life was despaired of, and Aunt Cassandra and my Father were summoned to the house—*there,* for a day or two, they hourly expected his death—but a favourable turn came, and he began to recover—My Father then went home. Aunt Cass. stayed on nearly a month, and Aunt Jane remained some weeks longer, to nurse the convalescent—

It was during this stay in London, that a little gleam of Court favor shone upon her. She had at first published her novels with a great desire of remaining *herself* unknown—but it was found impossible to preserve a secret that so many of the family knew and by this time, she had given up the attempt—and her name had been made public enough—tho' it was never inserted in the title page—

Two of the great Physicians of the day had attended my Uncle during his illness—I am not, at this distance of time, sufficiently sure *which* they were, as to give their names, but *one* of them had very intimate access to the Prince Regent, and continuing his visits during my Uncle's recovery, he told my Aunt one day, that the Prince was a great admirer of her novels: that he often read them, and had a set in each of his residences—That *he*, the physician had told his Royal Highness that Miss Austen was now in London, and that by the Prince's desire, Mr. Clarke, the Librarian of Carlton House, would speedily wait upon her—

Mr. Clarke came, and endorsed all previous compliments, and invited my Aunt to see Carlton House, saying the Prince had charged him to show her the Library there, adding many civilities as to the pleasure his R.H. had received from her novels—Three had then been published—The invitation could not be declined—and my Aunt went, at an appointed time, to Carlton House—

She saw the Library, and I beleive, some other apartments, but the particulars of her visit, if I ever heard them, I have now forgotten—only *this*, I *do* well recollect—that in the course of it, Mr. Clarke, speaking again of the Regent's admiration of her writing, declared himself charged to say, that if Miss Austen had any other novel forthcoming, she was quite at liberty to dedicate it to the Prince.

My Aunt made all proper acknowledgments at the moment, but had no intention of accepting the honor offered—until she was avised [*sic*] by some of her friends that she must consider the permission as a command—

Emma was then in the Publisher's hands—so a few lines of dedication were affixed to the 1st volume, and following still the instructions of the well informed, she sent a copy, handsomely bound, to Carlton House—and I *suppose* it was duly acknowledged by Mr. Clarke—

My Aunt, soon after her visit to *him*, returned home, where the little adventure was talked of for a while with some interest, and afforded some amusement—In the following Spring, Mr. Henry Austen ceased to reside in London, and my Aunt was never brought so near the precints of the Court again—nor did she ever try to recall herself to the recollection of Physician, Librarian or Prince, and so ended this little burst of Royal Patronage.

I beleive Aunt Jane's health began to fail some time before we knew she was really ill—but she became avowedly less equal to exercise. In a letter to me she says:

"I have taken one ride on the donkey and I like it very much, and you must try to get me quiet mild days that I may be able to go out pretty constantly—a great deal of wind does not suit me, as I have still a tendency to rheumatism. In short, I am but a poor Honey at present—I will be better when you can come and see us."—

A donkey carriage had been set up for my Grandmother's accomodation—but I think *she* seldom used it, and Aunt Jane found it a help to herself in getting to Alton—where, for a time, Capt. Austen had a house, after removing from his Brother's place at Chawton.—

In my later visits to Chawton Cottage, I remember Aunt Jane used often to lie down after dinner—My Grandmother herself was frequently on the sofa—sometimes in the afternoon, sometimes in the evening, at no fixed period of the day,—She had not bad health for her age, and she worked often for hours in the garden, and naturally wanted rest afterwards—There was only one sofa in the room—and Aunt Jane laid upon 3 chairs which she arranged for herself—I think she had a pillow, but it never looked comfortable—She called it *her* sofa, and even when the *other* was unoccupied, *she* never took it—It seemed understood that she preferred the chairs—

I wondered and wondered—for the real sofa was frequently vacant, and *still* she laid in this comfortless manner—I often asked her how she *could* like the chairs best—and I suppose I worried her into telling me the reason of her choice—which was, that if she ever used the sofa, Grandmama would be leaving it for her, and would not lie down, as she did now, whenever she felt inclined—

In May, 1816 my two Aunts went for a few weeks to Cheltenham—I am able to ascertain the date of this, and some similar occurrences by a reference to old pocket books in my possession—It was a journey in those days, to go from Hampshire into Gloucestershire and their first stage was to Steventon—They stayed one whole day, and left my Cousin Cassy to remain with us during their absence—

They made also a short stay at Mr. Fowle's at Kintbury I believe *that* was, as they returned—Mrs. Dexter, then Mary Jane Fowle, told me afterwards, that Aunt Jane went over the old places, and recalled old recollections associated with them, in a very particular manner—looked at them, my cousin thought, as if she never expected to see them again—The Kintbury family, during that visit, received an impression that her health was failing—altho' they did not know of any particular malady.

The year 1817, the last of my Aunt's life, began it seems under good auspices.

I copy from a letter of her's to myself dated Jany. 23rd—1817—the only letter I have which *does* bear the date of the year—

"I feel myself getting stronger than I was—and can so perfectly well walk to Alton, *or* back again, without the slightest fatigue that I hope to be able to do *both*, when summer comes—"

I do not know *when* the alarming symptoms of her malady came on—It was in the following March that I had the first idea of her being seriously ill—It had been settled that about the end of that month, or the beginning of April, I should spend a few days at Chawton, in the absence of my Father and Mother, who were just then engaged with Mrs. Leigh Perrot in arranging her late husband's affairs—it was shortly after Mr. Leigh Perrot's death—but Aunt Jane became too ill to have me in the house, and so I went instead to my sister, Mrs. Lefroy, at Wyards—The next day we walked over to Chawton to make enquiries after our Aunt—She was keeping her room but said she would see us, and we went up to her—She was in her dressing gown and was sitting quite like an invalide in an arm chair—but she got up, and kindly greeted us—and then pointing to seats which had been arranged for us by the fire, she said, "There's a chair for the married lady, and a little stool for you, Caroline."—It is strange, but those trifling words are the last of her's that I can remember—for I retain *no* recollection *at* all of what was said by any one in the conversation that of course ensued—

I was struck by the alteration in herself—She was very pale—her voice was weak and low and there was about her, a general appearance of debility and suffering; but I have been told that she never *had* much actual pain—

She was not equal to the exertion of talking to us, and our visit to the sick room was a very short one—Aunt Cassandra soon taking us away—I do not suppose we stayed a quarter of an hour; and *I* never saw Aunt Jane again—

I think she must have been particularly ill that day, and that in some degree she afterwards rallied—*I* soon went home again—but I beleive Mrs. Lefroy saw her more than once afterwards before she went to Winchester—

It was sometime in the following May, that she removed thither—Better medical advice was needed, than Alton could supply—Not I beleive with much hope that any skill could effect a cure but from the natural desire of her family to place her in the best hands—Mr. Lyford was thought to be very clever so much so, as to be generally summoned far beyond his own practise—to give his opinion in cases of serious illness—

In the earlier stages of her malady, my Aunt had had the advice, in London, of one of the eminent physicians of the day—

Aunt Cassandra, of course, accompanied her sister and they had lodgings in College Street—Their great friends Mrs. Heathcote and Miss Bigg, then living in The Close, had made all the arrangements for them, and did all they could to promote their comfort during that melancholy sojourn in Winchester.

Mr. Lyford could give no hope of recovery—He told my Mother that the duration of the illness must be very uncertain—it *might* be lingering or it might, with equal probability come to a sudden close—and that he feared the last period, whenever it arrived, would be one of severe suffering—but *this* was mercifully ordered otherwise—My mother, after a little time, had joined her sisters-in-law—to make it more cheerful for them, and also to take a share in the necessary attendance—From *her,* therefore, I learned, that my Aunt's resignation and composure of spirit were such, as those who knew her well, would have hoped for and expected—She was a humble and beleiving Christian; her life had passed in the cheerful performance of all home duties, and with *no* aiming at applause, she had sought, as if by instinct to promote the happiness of all those who came within her influence—doubtless she had her reward, in the peace of mind which was granted to her in her last days—

She was quite aware of her own danger—it was no delusive hope that kept up her spirits—and there was everything to attach her to life—Tho' she had passed by the hopes and enjoyments of youth, yet its sorrows also were left behind—and Autumn is sometimes so calm and fair that it consoles us for the departure of Spring and Summer—and *thus* it might have been with *her*—She was happy in her family and in her home, and no doubt the exercise of her great talent, was a happiness also in itself—and she was just learning to feel confidence in her own success—In no human mind was there less of vanity than in her's—yet she could not but be pleased and gratified as her works, by slow degrees made their way in the world, with constantly increasing favour—

She had *no* cause to be weary of life, and there was much to make it very pleasant to her—We may be sure she would fain have lived on—yet she was enabled, without complaint, and without dismay, to prepare for death—She had for some time known that it *might* be approaching her; and *now* she saw it with certainty, to be very near at hand.

The religious services most suitable to her state were ministered to her, during this, the last stage of her illness—sometimes by a Brother—Two of them were Clergymen and at Winchester she was within easy distance of both—

Her sweetness of temper never failed her; she was considerate and grateful to those who attended on her, and at times, when feeling rather better, her playfulness of spirit prevailed, and she amused them even in their sadness—A Brother frequently went over for a few hours, or a day or two—

Suddenly she became much worse—Mr. Lyford thought the

end was near at hand, and she beleived *herself* to be dying—and under this conviction she said all that she wished to say to those around her—

In taking then, as she thought, a last leave of my Mother, she thanked her for being there, and said, "You have always been a kind sister to me, Mary."—Contrary to any expectation, the immediate danger passed away; she became comfortable again, and seemed really better—

My Mother then came home—but not for long, as she was shortly summoned back—This was from no increase of my Aunt's illness, but because the Nurse could not be trusted for *her* share of the night attendance, having been more than once found asleep—so to relieve her from that part of her charge, Aunt Cassandra and my Mother and my Aunt's maid took the nights between them.

Aunt Jane continued very cheerfully and comfortable, and there began to be a *hope* of, at least, a respite from death—

But soon, and suddenly, as it were, a great change came on—*not* apparently, attended with much suffering—she sank rapidly—Mr. Lyford—when he saw her, could give no further hope, and she must have felt her own state—for when he asked her if there was anything she wanted, she replied, "Nothing but death." Those were her last words—

They watched by her through the night, and in quietness and peace she breathed her last on the morning of the 18th of July, 1817—

I need scarcely say she was dearly loved by her family—Her Brothers were very proud of her—Her literary fame, at the close of her life, was only just spreading—but they were proud of her talents, which *they* even then estimated highly—proud of her home virtues, of her cheerful spirit—of her pleasant looks—and *each* loved afterwards to *fancy* a resemblance in some daughter of his own, to the dear "Aunt Jane", whose perfect equal they *yet* never expected to see—

March 1867—Written out,
At Frog Firle—Sussex.

The donkey cart, known as 'Jane's Cart', shown after restoration.

RECOLLECTIONS OF JOHN WHITE

Foreword

John White, 1821–1921, lived at Chawton all his life. He was an agricultural labourer. He dictated the following Recollections to his daughter shortly before his death.

Edward Knight was Jane Austen's brother who became Knight in 1812.

"Mr. Papillion" was the Rev. John Papillon, Rector of Chawton, 1802–1836.

William Littleworth was no doubt of the same family as J. Littleworth and perhaps as Nanny Littlewart.

"Miss Prowten at Prowten Farm" was Miss Prowting, Jane Austen's friend. The house, part of which is still standing, was known in the Austens' day as "Prowtings". It is separated from Chawton Cottage by a large meadow, and villagers used to see Jane Austen climbing the stile at the bottom of her garden and crossing the field to visit the Prowting family. All these names, except that of William Littleworth, are mentioned in Jane Austen's Letters.

The house John White calls Chawton Cottage is not the Austens' but one nearly opposite, which has been so called for the past fifty years at least.

The riots he mentions occurred in 1830. They were especially formidable at Selborne, where the vicar capitulated to the mob, and promised to reduce the tithes.

The Recollections are now the property of the Chawton Women's Institute, whose kindness in giving permission to print them here is gratefully acknowledged by the Committee of the Jane Austen Society.

D. D.
E. J.

1952.

Recollections of John White, who died in 1921 at the age of one hundred.

My first recollections of Chawton are when I was about seven years old.

Mr. Edward Knight was the Squire.

The entrance to the coach road leading to Chawton House was at the Pasture Gate, opposite the Malt House Cottages.

Mr. Pillion (or Papillion) was the Rector before Mr. Charles Knight, "the Squire's brother".

William Carter was the Church clerk, and played the bassoon. There were four singers:—

The old George Pullinger (grandfather of the late G. Pullinger), Edmund Chandler, Stephen Boycey, and William Arnold.

The clerk and singers sat in the front gallery, the boys and sexton in the back gallery. The congregation did not join much in the singing and responses. Mrs. Knight had a singing master to teach the school children to sing the hymns in church. The master's name was Giffin.

Lady Bradford, (then Miss Knight), and William Shilton first trained a choir of men and boys.

Miss Cassandra Austen lived at the corner house by the Pond. She took a great interest in young girls, and taught them reading, the catechism and sewing. I remember a nice dog, his name was "Link", that she had. He always went with her manservant, William Littleworth, to Chawton House for milk, and carried it home in his mouth.

The school was where the Turners are living now, the schoolmistress was Mrs. Sarah Gibbs. She only taught some reading. Those that could had to go to Alton school to learn writing. I could not go, my father, being wounded at the time of the Battle of Waterloo, was often not able to work. I had to help earn a living for a large family instead of going to school.

James Goodchild's father, William Goodchild, (the sexton) had a class of sixteen boys for Sunday School. He lived in the cottage that Frederick Stacey has, there wasn't room for more than sixteen.

Captain Clements lived at the Dower House.

Mr. Hinton and Mrs. Ventress at Chawton Lodge.

Miss Prowten at Prowten Farm.

Chawton Cottage was then two small cottages.

Farmer Wickham is the first I remember at Pound Farm, after him Farmer Knight, then Mr. William Clements.

Farmer Wakes had the New Park Farm, after him Farmer Warren, Farmer Penny and Farmer Walton.

Farmer Spencer had the Old Park Farm, after him his son, William Spencer, then the grandson, William Spencer, of Wivelrod.

Before the railroad opened there were three coaches passed through for travellers, two from Winchester, one from Portsmouth. The morning coach from Winchester had six horses, the evening one four. The Portsmouth coach passed about mid-day. There was a road waggon for luggage, or passengers that could not pay coach fare.

People could not at first believe that coaches could be made to run without horses.

William Arnold, the church singer, was postman. Letters were not stamped then, but twopence had to be paid on delivery, a penny for postmaster and a penny for postman.

There was dancing and sports on May Day on the Butts Green.

There was a Cherry Fair held at the Four Marks every year. Everyone that could used to go to buy cherries and for the fun.

There was a Cheese Fair on Nore Hill once a year, where shopkeepers and farmers that didn't make their own used to get their supply for the year. We also had to go to Winchester for coal before the railroad was opened, and the principal marketing was done there or at Farnham. There was only a very small market in Alton.

The matches we used were flat pieces of wood dipped in brimstone. We had a flint stone, a piece of steel and tinder to set light to them.

Rioting broke out suddenly all over the country on account of dear food and small wages. Soldiers had to be called out, which soon stopped it, but not until a good deal of damage had been done, and the farmers promised better pay.

Selborne workhouse was quite destroyed.

Queen Victoria was crowned on my seventeenth birthday. There was a feast and amusements in Alton for the people. Tables were laid by the side of the pavement up the High Street.

In the year 1841 there were several Chawton young men emigrated to New Zealand. They were five months on the way and nearly all their children died on the voyage.

The front door of Jane Austen's house used to open straight into a room, but cannot recollect whether it was the dining room or the drawing room. The partition was put up afterwards when the house was turned into cottages for labourers.